# NOVEL NOTES

## A Writing Journal

Presented by Alex Apostol and

### FLOURISH & BLOG

*This journal is for all authors brave enough to venture into the world of writing*

**Novel Notes: A Writing Journal**

ISBN: 978-1516893454

# A little bit about

Alex Apostol

An Amazon bestselling author of Mythology, Alex Apostol writes in various genres of fiction. Her books can be found online at Amazon and Barnes & Nobel. Originally from northwest Indiana, she has lived all over the country in the last ten years, from Virginia to Hawaii. She currently lives in Texas with her husband, daughter, and two cats, Bob and Belle.

# NOVEL NOTES

*A Writing Journal*

# MY NOVEL'S TITLE

## MY NOVEL'S SUBTITLE

### MY NOVEL'S SERIES TITLE

# Planning Your Novel

Characters

World and Settings

Outline

Inspirations

# My Characters

### And their relationships

# Is Your Character Confident or Insecure

These two traits can influence your characters actions greatly, so take the time to figure out which one they are.

Confident People:
1. Give Compliments
2. Learn from Others
3. Take Responsibility
4. Operate on Principles
5. Admit mistakes
6. Show their Flaws
7. Positive
8. Risk-takers
9. Don't Talk Negative About Others
10. Givers
11. Like to Spend Time With Others
12. Accepts Others Differences
13. Can Laugh at Themselves
14. Make Decisions Quickly
15. Continue to Learn and Grow

Insecure People:

1. Closed Mindset
2. Constantly Seeks Validation
3. Act Like a Know-It-All
4. Always Makes Excuses
5. Does Only What Feels Good
6. Blames Others
7. Comes Across as Fake
8. Hide Flaws
9. Negative Thinker
10. Stays in Comfort Zone
11. Gossips
12. Taker
13. Dislikes Other People
14. Judgmental
15. Worries About What Others Think
16. Can't Make Decisions
17. Stays Stuck in Old Ways and Habits

These rules of Confident and Secure people are guidelines only. Some people, though, can share traits from both categories if they are seeking to change themselves in some way.

# Getting to Know Your Characters on a Psychological Level
## Distorted Ways of Thinking

<u>Filtering:</u> They take the negative details and magnify them while filtering out all the positive aspects of a situation. Example: Author thinks they're a failure because they only had two sales in one month, forgetting that they had those two sales which brought them two new loyal readers.

<u>Polarized Thinking:</u> Things are black and white, good or bad, you're perfect or a failure. There's no middle ground. Example: Reader found one typo in a book so they think it's a bad book.

<u>Overgeneralization:</u> You come to a general conclusion based on a single incident or piece of evidence. Example: If something bad happens then you expect it to happen again and again.

<u>Mind Reading:</u> Without their saying so, you know what people are feeling and why they act the way they do. In particular, you are able to divine how people are feeling about you. Example: Author thinks a reader doesn't like them because they didn't sign up for their mailing list when they bought a book.

<u>Castastrophizing:</u> Yes, it's a word and it means you expect disaster. You notice or hear about a problem and start with the "What Ifs". Example: Author doesn't put out the book they wrote because they're scared it won't sell.

*Personalization:* You think everything people say or do is in some kind of reaction to you. You also compare yourself to others, trying to determine who's smarter, better looking, ect. Example: Author thinks they suck because they're not as good a writer as J.K. Rowling.

*Control Fallacies:* If you feel extremely controlled, you see yourself as helpless or a victim of fate. The fallacy of internal control has you responsible for the pain and happiness of everyone around you. Example: Being a bestselling author is all luck and that's why I'm not one.

*Blaming:* You hold others responsible for your pain, or take the other tack and blame yourself for everything. Example: I can't help my family, because I can't sell books, because I'm a terrible writer and marketer, and it's all my fault we're struggling.

*Should:* You have an iron clad list of rules about how you and others should act. People who break the rules anger you and you feel guilty if you violate the rules. Examples: If one of your friends or family members don't buy your books then you get mad.

*Emotional Reasoning:* You believe what you feel must be true automatically. Example: If you feel stupid then you must be stupid.

*Fallacy of Change:* You expect others to change to suit you if you pressure them enough. You need to change people because your hope for happiness seem to depend entirely on them. Example: We're all thinking it. Girlfriend tries to changer her boyfriend.

Global Labeling: You generalize one or two qualities into a negative global judgement. Examples: Racism is the first one that comes to mind for me.

Being Right: You are continually on trial to prove that your opinions and actions are correct. Example: Being wrong is unthinkable and you will go to any length to prove you're right.

Heaven's Reward Fallacy: You expect all your sacrifices and self-denial to pay off, as if there were someone keeping score. You feel bitter when that reward doesn't come. Example: Religion.

It's important to remember that real people do not have just one distorted way of thinking and neither should your characters. My characters have anywhere between three and seven different ones! This will make your characters seem more real to your readers.

# Personality Types

Extravert: These people have high energy, talk more than listen, think out loud, act first and then think later, prefer a public role, can get easily distracted, prefer to do lots of things at once, are outgoing and enthusiastic.

Introverts: They have quiet energy, listen more than talk, think quietly inside their heads, think then act, feel comfortable being alone, prefer to work behind-the-scenes, have good powers of concentration, prefer to focus on one thing at a time, self-contained and reserved.

Sensors: They focus on details and specifics, admire practical solutions, notice details, remember facts, pragmatic- see "what is", live in the here and now, trust actual experiences, like to use established skills, like step-by-step instructions, work at a steady pace.

Intuitives: These people focus on the big picture and possibilities, admire creative ideas, notice anything new or different, inventive- see what could be, think about future implications, trust their gut instincts, prefer to learn new skills, like to figure things out for themselves, work in bursts of energy.

Feelers: Decide based on feelings, appear warm and friendly, are convinced by how they feel, are diplomatic and tactful, value harmony and compassion, take many things personally, are quick to compliment others, are motivated by appreciation, avoid arguments and conflict.

_Thinkers:_ Make decisions objectively, appear cool and reserved, convinced by rational arguments, honest and direct, value honesty and fairness, take few things personally, good at seeing flaws, motivated by achievement, argue or debate issues for fun.

_Perceivers:_ They like to keep their options open, playful and casual, less aware of time, may run late, prefer to start projects, play first and then work later, have difficulty making decisions, questions the need for many rules, likes to keep plans flexible, want the freedom to be spontaneous.

_Judgers:_ They like to have things settled, take responsibilities seriously, pay attention to time and usually prompt, prefer to finish projects, work first then play later, seek closure, see the need for most rules, like to make and stick to plans, find comfort in schedules.

These categories of personality types, like most psychological categories, are not set in stone. Your character does not have to embody every single thing listed under a type. But these are majorities for those types of personalities. I tend to write my character for a while, maybe even the entire book, and then decide which one they are and edit where they are not being true to their main personality type, though a character can be more than one. They will always have a primary type, though.

# Is Your Character Toxic or Not?

Traits of a Toxic Person:

1. They'll keep you guessing about which version of them you're getting.
2. They manipulate.
3. They won't own their feelings, but project them on you.
4. They'll make you prove yourself to them and will regularly put you in a position to choose between them and something else.
5. They never apologize.
6. They'll be there in a crisis, but they'll never share in your joy.
7. They'll leave a conversation unfinished and then go "offline".
8. They'll use non-toxic words with a toxic tone.
9. They'll bring irrelevant details into a conversation or argument.
10. They'll make it about the way you're talking rather than what you're talking about.
11. They exaggerate.
12. They are judgmental.

This list came in handy while I was writing Dead Soil, where I created characters specifically to be toxic in nature. Every zombie survival series needs toxic people. In real life, we always come across them whether we know it or not at the time.

# The Hero's Journey

This is a list that has become very popular with writers. I don't tend to stick to it, but I think my characters of Dead Soil embody this the most, and I even added a new character just to round out the journey list.

<u>The Hero:</u> The unassuming regular guy or girl who finds themselves cast in a new world.

<u>The Sidekick:</u> A kind soul who stays by the hero's side. Then leaves. Then returns to save the day.

<u>The Mentor:</u> Points the way as far as they can and then dies.

<u>The Princess:</u> The woman with vision, insight, and the keys. Love interest.

<u>The Gentle Giant:</u> Initially fearsome, proves to have a heart as oversized as their body.

<u>The Comic Duo:</u> Bumbling twins who never quite seem to get it right. (until they prove themselves in the end.)

<u>The Villain:</u> The one true face of evil. The one the hero must destroy.

<u>The Villain's Army:</u> Inhuman and endless in numbers.

# The Character Worksheet

This is the design I used in my own notebook while I was developing Dead Soil: A Zombie Series. I like to get to know my characters as deeply as I can so they take on a life of their own, doing things that sometimes even surprise me! The Quick Profiles are great for when you're adding in a small background fact such as where they work or their age. The open space for appearance is great because I never know how detailed I will get when describing a character, which is why I did not line that area. You can draw them out if you're artistically inclines, or bullet quick facts like hair color, eye color, skin color, ect. I have also added in the psychological traits and personalities for you to dig deep and learn to think how your character thinks, even the most despicable and toxic ones! While you're working on these, though, remember that characters, like people, develop and change. Just because your character started out as a non-toxic introvert does not mean they will not develop into a rude, obnoxious, toxic, extrovert later on in the novel or series! Continually update your character profiles!

# Quick Bio

Full Name:
Age:
Born In:
Currently Lives In:
Occupation:
Hobbies:
Relationship Status:
Hair Color and Length:
Eye Color and Shape:
Height:
Weight:
Body Build:
Skin Color/Heritage:
Distinguishing Marks:
Tattoos:
Personality Traits:

# A Brief History

# Continued History:

# More On Appearance:

# Psychological:

#1 Motivator:

Hero's Journey Role:

Toxic or Non-Toxic:

Personality Type:

Distorted Ways of Thinking:

Confident or Insecure:

# Quick Bio

Full Name:
Age:
Born In:
Currently Lives In:
Occupation:
Hobbies:
Relationship Status:
Hair Color and Length:
Eye Color and Shape:
Height:
Weight:
Body Build:
Skin Color/Heritage:
Distinguishing Marks:
Tattoos:
Personality Traits:

# A Brief History

# Continued History:

# More On Appearance:

# Psychological:

#1 Motivator:

Hero's Journey Role:

Toxic or Non-Toxic:

Personality Type:

Distorted Ways of Thinking:

Confident or Insecure:

# Quick Bio

Full Name:

Age:

Born In:

Currently Lives In:

Occupation:

Hobbies:

Relationship Status:

Hair Color and Length:

Eye Color and Shape:

Height:

Weight:

Body Build:

Skin Color/Heritage:

Distinguishing Marks:

Tattoos:

Personality Traits:

# A Brief History

# Continued History:


# More On Appearance:


# Psychological:

#1 Motivator:

Hero's Journey Role:

Toxic or Non-Toxic:

Personality Type:

Distorted Ways of Thinking:

Confident or Insecure:

# Quick Bio

Full Name:
Age:
Born In:
Currently Lives In:
Occupation:
Hobbies:
Relationship Status:
Hair Color and Length:
Eye Color and Shape:
Height:
Weight:
Body Build:
Skin Color/Heritage:
Distinguishing Marks:
Tattoos:
Personality Traits:

# A Brief History

# Continued History:

# More On Appearance:

# Psychological:

#1 Motivator:

Hero's Journey Role:

Toxic or Non-Toxic:

Personality Type:

Distorted Ways of Thinking:

Confident or Insecure:

## Quick Bio

Full Name:
Age:
Born In:
Currently Lives In:
Occupation:
Hobbies:
Relationship Status:
Hair Color and Length:
Eye Color and Shape:
Height:
Weight:
Body Build:
Skin Color/Heritage:
Distinguishing Marks:
Tattoos:
Personality Traits:

## A Brief History

# Continued History:

# More On Appearance:

# Psychological:

#1 Motivator:

Hero's Journey Role:

Toxic or Non-Toxic:

Personality Type:

Distorted Ways of Thinking:

Confident or Insecure:

# Quick Bio

Full Name:
Age:
Born In:
Currently Lives In:
Occupation:
Hobbies:
Relationship Status:
Hair Color and Length:
Eye Color and Shape:
Height:
Weight:
Body Build:
Skin Color/Heritage:
Distinguishing Marks:
Tattoos:
Personality Traits:

# A Brief History

# Continued History:

# More On Appearance:

# Psychological:

#1 Motivator:

Hero's Journey Role:

Toxic or Non-Toxic:

Personality Type:

Distorted Ways of Thinking:

Confident or Insecure:

# Quick Bio

Full Name:
Age:
Born In:
Currently Lives In:
Occupation:
Hobbies:
Relationship Status:
Hair Color and Length:
Eye Color and Shape:
Height:
Weight:
Body Build:
Skin Color/Heritage:
Distinguishing Marks:
Tattoos:
Personality Traits:

# A Brief History

# Continued History:

# More On Appearance:

# Psychological:

#1 Motivator:

Hero's Journey Role:

Toxic or Non-Toxic:

Personality Type:

Distorted Ways of Thinking:

Confident or Insecure:

# Quick Bio

Full Name:
Age:
Born In:
Currently Lives In:
Occupation:
Hobbies:
Relationship Status:
Hair Color and Length:
Eye Color and Shape:
Height:
Weight:
Body Build:
Skin Color/Heritage:
Distinguishing Marks:
Tattoos:
Personality Traits:

# A Brief History

# Continued History:

# More On Appearance:

# Psychological:

#1 Motivator:

Hero's Journey Role:

Toxic or Non-Toxic:

Personality Type:

Distorted Ways of Thinking:

Confident or Insecure:

# Quick Bio

Full Name:
Age:
Born In:
Currently Lives In:
Occupation:
Hobbies:
Relationship Status:
Hair Color and Length:
Eye Color and Shape:
Height:
Weight:
Body Build:
Skin Color/Heritage:
Distinguishing Marks:
Tattoos:
Personality Traits:

# A Brief History

# Continued History:

# More On Appearance:

# Psychological:

#1 Motivator:

Hero's Journey Role:

Toxic or Non-Toxic:

Personality Type:

Distorted Ways of Thinking:

Confident or Insecure:

## Quick Bio

Full Name:
Age:
Born In:
Currently Lives In:
Occupation:
Hobbies:
Relationship Status:
Hair Color and Length:
Eye Color and Shape:
Height:
Weight:
Body Build:
Skin Color/Heritage:
Distinguishing Marks:
Tattoos:
Personality Traits:

## A Brief History

## Continued History:

## More On Appearance:

## Psychological:

#1 Motivator:

Hero's Journey Role:

Toxic or Non-Toxic:

Personality Type:

Distorted Ways of Thinking:

Confident or Insecure:

# Quick Bio

Full Name:
Age:
Born In:
Currently Lives In:
Occupation:
Hobbies:
Relationship Status:
Hair Color and Length:
Eye Color and Shape:
Height:
Weight:
Body Build:
Skin Color/Heritage:
Distinguishing Marks:
Tattoos:
Personality Traits:

# A Brief History

# Continued History:

# More On Appearance:

# Psychological:

#1 Motivator:

Hero's Journey Role:

Toxic or Non-Toxic:

Personality Type:

Distorted Ways of Thinking:

Confident or Insecure:

# Quick Bio

Full Name:
Age:
Born In:
Currently Lives In:
Occupation:
Hobbies:
Relationship Status:
Hair Color and Length:
Eye Color and Shape:
Height:
Weight:
Body Build:
Skin Color/Heritage:
Distinguishing Marks:
Tattoos:
Personality Traits:

# A Brief History

## Continued History:

## More On Appearance:

## Psychological:

#1 Motivator:

Hero's Journey Role:

Toxic or Non-Toxic:

Personality Type:

Distorted Ways of Thinking:

Confident or Insecure:

# Quick Bio

Full Name:
Age:
Born In:
Currently Lives In:
Occupation:
Hobbies:
Relationship Status:
Hair Color and Length:
Eye Color and Shape:
Height:
Weight:
Body Build:
Skin Color/Heritage:
Distinguishing Marks:
Tattoos:
Personality Traits:

# A Brief History

# Continued History:

# More On Appearance:

# Psychological:

#1 Motivator:

Hero's Journey Role:

Toxic or Non-Toxic:

Personality Type:

Distorted Ways of Thinking:

Confident or Insecure:

# Quick Bio

Full Name:
Age:
Born In:
Currently Lives In:
Occupation:
Hobbies:
Relationship Status:
Hair Color and Length:
Eye Color and Shape:
Height:
Weight:
Body Build:
Skin Color/Heritage:
Distinguishing Marks:
Tattoos:
Personality Traits:

# A Brief History

# Continued History:


# More On Appearance:


# Psychological:

#1 Motivator:

Hero's Journey Role:

Toxic or Non-Toxic:

Personality Type:

Distorted Ways of Thinking:

Confident or Insecure:

# Quick Bio

Full Name:
Age:
Born In:
Currently Lives In:
Occupation:
Hobbies:
Relationship Status:
Hair Color and Length:
Eye Color and Shape:
Height:
Weight:
Body Build:
Skin Color/Heritage:
Distinguishing Marks:
Tattoos:
Personality Traits:

# A Brief History

# Continued History:

# More On Appearance:

# Psychological:

#1 Motivator:

Hero's Journey Role:

Toxic or Non-Toxic:

Personality Type:

Distorted Ways of Thinking:

Confident or Insecure:

# Quick Bio

Full Name:
Age:
Born In:
Currently Lives In:
Occupation:
Hobbies:
Relationship Status:
Hair Color and Length:
Eye Color and Shape:
Height:
Weight:
Body Build:
Skin Color/Heritage:
Distinguishing Marks:
Tattoos:
Personality Traits:

# A Brief History

# Continued History:

# More On Appearance:

# Psychological:

#1 Motivator:

Hero's Journey Role:

Toxic or Non-Toxic:

Personality Type:

Distorted Ways of Thinking:

Confident or Insecure:

# Quick Bio

Full Name:
Age:
Born In:
Currently Lives In:
Occupation:
Hobbies:
Relationship Status:
Hair Color and Length:
Eye Color and Shape:
Height:
Weight:
Body Build:
Skin Color/Heritage:
Distinguishing Marks:
Tattoos:
Personality Traits:

# A Brief History

# Continued History:

# More On Appearance:

# Psychological:

#1 Motivator:

Hero's Journey Role:

Toxic or Non-Toxic:

Personality Type:

Distorted Ways of Thinking:

Confident or Insecure:

# Quick Bio

Full Name:
Age:
Born In:
Currently Lives In:
Occupation:
Hobbies:
Relationship Status:
Hair Color and Length:
Eye Color and Shape:
Height:
Weight:
Body Build:
Skin Color/Heritage:
Distinguishing Marks:
Tattoos:
Personality Traits:

# A Brief History

# Continued History:

# More On Appearance:

# Psychological:

#1 Motivator:

Hero's Journey Role:

Toxic or Non-Toxic:

Personality Type:

Distorted Ways of Thinking:

Confident or Insecure:

# Quick Bio

Full Name:
Age:
Born In:
Currently Lives In:
Occupation:
Hobbies:
Relationship Status:
Hair Color and Length:
Eye Color and Shape:
Height:
Weight:
Body Build:
Skin Color/Heritage:
Distinguishing Marks:
Tattoos:
Personality Traits:

# A Brief History

# Continued History:


# More On Appearance:


# Psychological:

#1 Motivator:

Hero's Journey Role:

Toxic or Non-Toxic:

Personality Type:

Distorted Ways of Thinking:

Confident or Insecure:

# Quick Bio

Full Name:
Age:
Born In:
Currently Lives In:
Occupation:
Hobbies:
Relationship Status:
Hair Color and Length:
Eye Color and Shape:
Height:
Weight:
Body Build:
Skin Color/Heritage:
Distinguishing Marks:
Tattoos:
Personality Traits:

# A Brief History

# Continued History:

# More On Appearance:

# Psychological:

#1 Motivator:

Hero's Journey Role:

Toxic or Non-Toxic:

Personality Type:

Distorted Ways of Thinking:

Confident or Insecure:

# Character Relationships

Pick two of your characters and give a brief description of their relationship. How did they meet? Are they friends or enemies?

# Character Relationships

Pick two of your characters and give a brief description of their relationship. How did they meet? Are they friends or enemies?

# Relationship Diagram

Here is an example from Alex Apostol's
Kamlyn Paige series

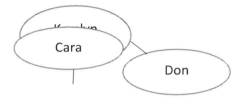

# Relationship Diagram Cont...

# My Novel's World

### And scene settings

# My World

These pages were intentionally left blank for you to create your world as you please. Draw a map, describe with words, whatever your process is!

# My World Cont...

My World Cont....

# My World Cont...

My World Cont...

My World Cont...

# My World Cont...

# My World Cont...

# My World Cont...

# My World Cont...

# Rules of My World

1.

2.

3.

4.

5.

6.

7.

8.

9.

10.

11.

12.

13.

14.

15.

16.

17.

18.

19.

20.

21.

22.

23.

24.

25.

26.

27.

# Scene Setting

*Describe the scene briefly and where it belongs in the story. This can be done after the outline is completed.*

# Scene Setting

Describe the scene briefly and where it belongs in the story. This can be done after the outline is completed.

# Scene Setting

Describe the scene briefly and where it belongs in the story. This can be done after the outline is completed.

# Scene Setting

*Describe the scene briefly and where it belongs in the story. This can be done after the outline is completed.*

# Scene Setting

*Describe the scene briefly and where it belongs in the story. This can be done after the outline is completed.*

# My Novel's Outline

Where the magic happens

# My Novel's Outline

Make sure your novel has direction before you actually start writing. An outline can be as brief as one word sections or as detailed as a paragraph.

Just don't get too carried away or you'll never start your novel!

# Example Outline

I. The Chapter- maybe include a brief overview of important event
  A. First event or scene
    1. Important detail of first event or scene
    2. Another important detail of first event or scene
      a. added detail to the details above
      b. added detail to the details above
  B. Second event or scene
    1. Important detail of second event or scene
      a. added detail to the details above
      b. added detail to the details above
    2. Important detail of second event or scene
II. Second Chapter

And so on and so forth, you get the idea. You don't have to follow this outline exactly. It is just the way I do mine when writing my novels.

# Now for YOUR outline

# My Novel's Outline

# My Novel's Outline

# My Novel's Outline

# My Novel's Outline

# My Novel's Outline

# My Novel's Outline

# My Novel's Outline

# My Novel's Outline

# My Novel's Outline

# My Novel's Outline

# My Novel's Outline

# My Novel's Outline

# My Novel's Outline

# My Novel's Outline

# My Novel's Outline

# My Novel's Outline

# My Novel's Outline

# My Novel's Outline

# My Novel's Outline

# My Novel's Outline

# My Novel's Outline

# My Novel's Outline

# My Novel's Outline

# My Novel's Outline

# My Novel's Outline

# My Novel's Outline

# My Novel's Outline

# My Novel's Outline

# My Novel's Outline

# My Novel's Outline

# My Novel's Outline

# My Novel's Outline

# My Novel's Outline

# My Novel's Outline

# My Novel's Outline

# My Novel's Outline

# My Novel's Outline

# My Novel's Outline

# My Novel's Outline

# My Novel's Outline

# My Novel's Outline

# My Novel's Outline

# My Novel's Outline

# My Novel's Outline

# My Novel's Outline

# My Novel's Outline

# My Novel's Outline

# My Novel's Outline

# My Novel's Outline

# My Novel's Outline

# My Novel's Outline

# My Novel's Outline

# My Novel's Outline

# My Novel's Outline

# My Novel's Outline

# My Novel's Outline

# My Novel's Outline

# My Novel's Outline

# My Novel's Outline

# My Novel's Outline

# My Novel's Outline

# My Novel's Outline

# My Novel's Outline

# My Novel's Outline

# My Novel's Outline

# My Novel's Outline

# My Novel's Outline

# My Novel's Outline

# My Novel's Outline

# My Novel's Outline

# My Novel's Outline

# My Novel's Outline

# My Novel's Outline

# My Novel's Outline

# My Novel's Outline

# My Novel's Outline

# My Novel's Outline

# My Novel's Outline

# My Novel's Outline

# My Novel's Outline

# My Novel's Outline

# My Novel's Outline

# My Novel's Outline

# My Novel's Outline

# My Novel's Outline

# My Novel's Outline

# My Novel's Outline

# My Novel's Outline

# My Novel's Outline

# My Novel's Outline

# My Novel's Outline

# My Novel's Outline

# My Novel's Outline

# My Novel's Outline

# My Novel's Outline

# My Novel's Outline

# My Novel's Outline

# My Novel's Outline

# My Novel's Outline

# My Novel's Outline

# My Inspiration

Consider singing up for Pinterest to gather inspirational photos. Make a board for each book and write a little teaser for the caption to the photo you've pinned. This will get people wondering about your book. Also, your photos are all right there if you want to write a character inspiration blog post for you upcoming novel, another great way to get readers interested in your novel while you're still writing it!

# Music Inspiration

# Music Inspiration

# Character Inspiration

# Character Inspiration

# Books that Inspired

# Books that Inspired

# Movies and TV Shows that Inspired

# Movies and TV Shows that Inspired

# Other Inspiration

# Other Inspiration

While

Writing

# My Writing Diary

A great place to vent your frustrations or celebrate an awesome day of writing your novel.

# My Writing Diary

This is a place for you to write daily how you feel about your writing for the day. Keep it brief and include a daily word count

## Example

WC: 1,831

Today was a pretty easy day, except I couldn't quite get the description for Kamlyn down right. A lot of time spent looking through the thesaurus.

A great place to start is your feelings. Do you feel accomplished? Disappointed? Eager to write again? Then describe why.

# My Writing Diary

Week #

Day 1 WC:

Day 2 WC:

Day 3 WC:

Day 4 WC:

Day 5 WC:

Day 6 WC:

Day 7 WC:

# My Writing Diary
### Week #

Day 1 WC:

Day 2 WC:

Day 3 WC:

Day 4 WC:

Day 5 WC:

Day 6 WC:

Day 7 WC:

# My Writing Diary

Week #

Day 1 WC:

Day 2 WC:

Day 3 WC:

Day 4 WC:

Day 5 WC:

Day 6 WC:

Day 7 WC:

# My Writing Diary

Week #

Day 1 WC:

Day 2 WC:

Day 3 WC:

Day 4 WC:

Day 5 WC:

Day 6 WC:

Day 7 WC:

# My Writing Diary
## Week #

Day 1 WC:

Day 2 WC:

Day 3 WC:

Day 4 WC:

Day 5 WC:

Day 6 WC:

Day 7 WC:

# My Writing Diary

Week #

Day 1 WC:

Day 2 WC:

Day 3 WC:

Day 4 WC:

Day 5 WC:

Day 6 WC:

Day 7 WC:

# My Writing Diary

Week #

Day 1 WC:

Day 2 WC:

Day 3 WC:

Day 4 WC:

Day 5 WC:

Day 6 WC:

Day 7 WC:

# My Writing Diary
Week #

Day 1 WC:

Day 2 WC:

Day 3 WC:

Day 4 WC:

Day 5 WC:

Day 6 WC:

Day 7 WC:

# My Writing Diary
Week #

Day 1 WC:

Day 2 WC:

Day 3 WC:

Day 4 WC:

Day 5 WC:

Day 6 WC:

Day 7 WC:

# My Writing Diary Week #

Day 1 WC:

Day 2 WC:

Day 3 WC:

Day 4 WC:

Day 5 WC:

Day 6 WC:

Day 7 WC:

# My Writing Diary

Week #

Day 1 WC:

Day 2 WC:

Day 3 WC:

Day 4 WC:

Day 5 WC:

Day 6 WC:

Day 7 WC:

# My Writing Diary

Week #

Day 1 WC:

Day 2 WC:

Day 3 WC:

Day 4 WC:

Day 5 WC:

Day 6 WC:

Day 7 WC:

# My Writing Diary

Week #

Day 1 WC:

Day 2 WC:

Day 3 WC:

Day 4 WC:

Day 5 WC:

Day 6 WC:

Day 7 WC:

# My Writing Diary

Week #

Day 1 WC:

Day 2 WC:

Day 3 WC:

Day 4 WC:

Day 5 WC:

Day 6 WC:

Day 7 WC:

# My Writing Diary

Week #

Day 1 WC:

Day 2 WC:

Day 3 WC:

Day 4 WC:

Day 5 WC:

Day 6 WC:

Day 7 WC:

# My Writing Diary

Week #

Day 1 WC:

Day 2 WC:

Day 3 WC:

Day 4 WC:

Day 5 WC:

Day 6 WC:

Day 7 WC:

# My Writing Diary

Week #

Day 1 WC:

Day 2 WC:

Day 3 WC:

Day 4 WC:

Day 5 WC:

Day 6 WC:

Day 7 WC:

# My Writing Diary
### Week #

Day 1 WC:

Day 2 WC:

Day 3 WC:

Day 4 WC:

Day 5 WC:

Day 6 WC:

Day 7 WC:

# My Writing Diary

Week #

Day 1 WC:

Day 2 WC:

Day 3 WC:

Day 4 WC:

Day 5 WC:

Day 6 WC:

Day 7 WC:

# My Writing Diary
Week #

Day 1 WC:

Day 2 WC:

Day 3 WC:

Day 4 WC:

Day 5 WC:

Day 6 WC:

Day 7 WC:

# My Writing Diary
### Week #

Day 1 WC:

Day 2 WC:

Day 3 WC:

Day 4 WC:

Day 5 WC:

Day 6 WC:

Day 7 WC:

# My Writing Diary
Week #

Day 1 WC:

Day 2 WC:

Day 3 WC:

Day 4 WC:

Day 5 WC:

Day 6 WC:

Day 7 WC:

# My Writing Diary

Week #

Day 1 WC:

Day 2 WC:

Day 3 WC:

Day 4 WC:

Day 5 WC:

Day 6 WC:

Day 7 WC:

# My Writing Diary

Week #

Day 1 WC:

Day 2 WC:

Day 3 WC:

Day 4 WC:

Day 5 WC:

Day 6 WC:

Day 7 WC:

# My Writing Diary

Week #

Day 1 WC:

Day 2 WC:

Day 3 WC:

Day 4 WC:

Day 5 WC:

Day 6 WC:

Day 7 WC:

# My Writing Diary
Week #

Day 1 WC:

Day 2 WC:

Day 3 WC:

Day 4 WC:

Day 5 WC:

Day 6 WC:

Day 7 WC:

# After Writing

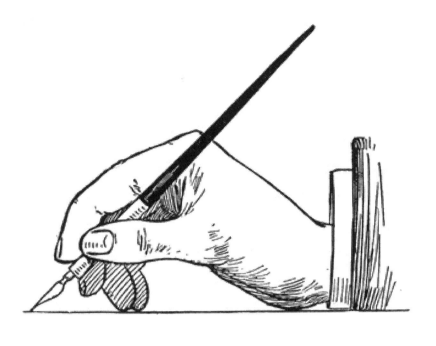

Social Media Log

Advertising Log

My Novel's Best Quotes

My Novel's Personal Info

Gains and Losses Ledger

# Social Media Log

A place to do your social media research

Record which types of posts work and what's the best time

to post. Pick your favorite sites and cut out the rest.

# Social Media Log

# Social Media Log

# Advertising Log

*Record who you purchase advertisment space from and for how much.*

# Advertising Log

# Advertising Log

# Your Novel's Best Quotes

## For Sharing

While you're reading through your novel, write down your favorite quotes to share with people in advertisements and on social media sites.

# Your Novel's Best Quotes

## For Sharing

# Your Novel's Best Quotes
## For Sharing

# My Novel's Personal Info

Official Title:

Official Subtitle:

Series Belonging To:

Book # in Series:

ASIN #

ISBN 10

ISBN 13

Publisher:

Published Through These Sites:

eBook Price $

Paperback Price $

Hardcover Price $

Audiobook Price $

Other Information:

# Gains and Losses

| Profits from Books Sold | Costs for Book & Marketing |
|---|---|
| $ | $ |

# Gains and Losses

| Profits from Books Sold | Costs for Book & Marketing |
|---|---|
| $ | $ |

# Gains and Losses

| Profits from Books Sold | Costs for Book & Marketing |
|---|---|
| $ | $ |

# Extra Blank Pages

# Extra Blank Pages

# Extra Blank Pages

# Extra Blank Pages

# Congratulations on Completing Your Novel

From                                    Alex Apostol and

## FLOURISH & BLOG

Don't forget to check out Alex Apostol's books on Amazon or her website

Authoralexapostol.com

Made in the USA
Middletown, DE
31 October 2016